SPIRITUAL RENEWAL

RELEASING RIVERS OF LIVING WATER

Studies by Paul H. Wilson

A **met** Publication

Published on behalf of MET by

MOORLEYS
Print, Design & Publishing
info@moorleys.co.uk · www.moorleys.co.uk

Published by
Methodist Evangelicals Together (MET)
ISBN 978 0 86071 894 9

First edition published in the United Kingdom 2022
©2022 MET

British Library Cataloguing in Publication Data.

A catalogue record of this book is available from
the British Library.

Unless otherwise stated, Scripture quotations are taken from
The Holy Bible, the New International Version
(Anglicised, Zondervan, 2011)

Contents

A Renewal Movement: Bible-Based & Prayer-Focussed

MET is a fellowship for every Methodist who:
- upholds the authority of scripture and the importance of prayer
- is committed to the centrality of the cross and the urgency of evangelism
- prays for revival and spiritual renewal

Our three core purposes are:
- **ADVOCATING:** promoting and representing evangelicalism within Methodism, and Wesleyan evangelicalism within the wider evangelical world
- **EQUIPPING:** providing resources through publications, conferences and our website for evangelicals within British Methodism
- **SUPPORTING:** offering pastoral support and advice to evangelicals, who can often feel isolated within Methodism and face particular pressures

Join MET and partner with us to:
- network with evangelical Methodists in prayer and action
- add your voice to many others on key issues at all levels of the Methodist Church and beyond
- participate in national and local events
- receive the MET Connexion Magazine

Find us at: www.methodistevangelicals.org.uk

Introduction

Where do you start in a series of Bible Studies on spiritual renewal? Perhaps it is to consider where you are on your spiritual journey. This series is an opportunity to seek spiritual renewal, to encounter God and recharge your spiritual batteries. Reading and reflecting on familiar and not-so-familiar stories in the Bible, praying individually, corporately, or with a ministry team in your local church, you may experience the gentle renewing ministry of God, Father, Son and Holy Spirit.

So much has happened to us in the last two years. Covid-19 was more than simply a virus. Whether we contracted it or not, Covid-19 may have affected us in so many different ways. The list for each of us is varied, but we must acknowledge its effects. Lock-down, illness, bereavement, delayed medical treatments or investigations, tiredness, and isolation from family, friends, colleagues, and church may have affected us differently. The pressures of juggling working from home and educating children, losing jobs, furlough, and supporting family, friends and neighbours are just a few more to add to the list. Others experienced release from church roles. While others took on different new tasks, facilitating hybrid worship, meetings and small groups. All of the above, plus the responsibilities of family, work and church that we were already carrying, have resulted in many being physically, mentally, emotionally and spiritually exhausted.

In prayerful preparation for this series, I began to take a detour from the original plan to an initial chapter looking at Elijah. He was a spiritual giant who won great victories but experienced burn out. God took him on a journey through the wilderness to a place of spiritual significance. There God met with and ministered to Elijah.

Throughout my ministry, I have experienced those moments when God has taken me from a spiritual low to a place of renewal and fruitful ministry.

Perhaps you have picked up this study series sometime after the Covid pandemic. Still, life events may have left you seeking the gentle renewing touch of God. We dare to respond to the invitation of Jesus:

> 'On the last and greatest day of the festival, Jesus stood and said in a loud voice, "Let anyone who is thirsty come to me and drink. Whoever believes in me, as Scripture has said, rivers of living water will flow from within them." By this he meant the Spirit, whom those who believed in him were later to receive. Up to that time the Spirit had not been given since Jesus had not yet been glorified.' (John 7:37-39)

Over many years, God used The Lay Witness Movement, predominantly within the Methodist Church, to bring spiritual renewal to many individuals and churches alike. It was a weekend where a team of lay people from various backgrounds and churches, joined a local church that wanted to take the next step with God.

I recall two exercises used to help people reflect on where they were with God at the start of the weekend. They allowed people to reflect and discern, 'What are you doing here?', God's question to Elijah on Mount Horeb (also known as Mount Sinai). Put another way, 'Where are you on your spiritual journey?'

One exercise was to take a piece of string to represent your life. The leader then invited you to think through key events that impacted your spiritual life. Placing knots along the string, some were very close, others further apart, you had a physical reminder of your life journey. Karen and I were on the Lay Witness teams for several years until I entered training for the Methodist Ministry. I remember using my piece of string to speak about several events in my life which impacted my spiritual journey. It enabled me to take stock of where I was on that journey and what the next steps might be. The exercise may help you stop and reflect upon those moments in your life when God has helped you, called you forward, picked you up, or been very real or seemingly absent. They may allow you to see times when you have moved away from God, through business, an argument in church, or the way someone has deeply hurt you. Perhaps the importance is to reflect upon where you are now in your relationship with God.

An alternative exercise on those Lay Witness weekends was to draw a timeline of your life, mapping your age, from left to right, and closeness to God, from bottom to top. A wavy line may emerge of peaks and troughs, reflecting times of spiritual growth, plateaus of constancy or times of falling away. Today, may be at a high or low point. It is another way of mapping your spiritual journey, showing the ups and downs of your walk with God. You will recall events which affected your closeness to God. Such an exercise allows an honest moment as to where you are now.

You may wish to take time to reflect on how you feel. What events have helped or hindered your walk with God? What do you need at present? Some may wish to share with a friend or take time to be honest with yourself and God about where you are now in your spiritual life.

For Reflection...

0.1. Where are you on your spiritual journey?

0.2. Use the string exercise above to help you think about your relationship with God at different times in your life.

0.3. Use the timeline exercise above and consider the spiritual highs and lows during your life.

1: Are You Weary?

1 Kings 17-19

As you reflect upon your spiritual journey or recent events, one word you may use to express how you feel is weary. You are not alone in feeling that way. Many people, after a time of extreme pressure, heavy workload, grief or caring for others, can feel that way. Spiritually, when the preacher or worship leader ends the service, they are often at their most spiritually vulnerable. We all need time to rest and recover. We need time to experience spiritual renewal. The Sabbath principle has been eroded in our culture. Even days off are filled with activity. Yet God placed the sabbath into the weekly timetable for a purpose.

The story of Elijah in 1 Kings 17-19 provides an opportunity to see an example of a spiritual hero who experienced spiritual highs and lows. It highlights God's grace in meeting Elijah's deepest needs. He needed a pick-me-up. We shall see God care for Elijah. We shall see how God cares for you and me.

Elijah's ministry took place in the 9th century before Christ. He breaks onto the scene in 1 Kings 17:1, *'Now Elijah the Tishbite, from Tishbe in Gilead, said to Ahab.'* He was an ordinary person used by God to do extraordinary things. The description 'Elijah the Tishbite' meant he was simply known by where he came from rather than what he had previously done. This seemingly ordinary person took on the prophetic role of calling King Ahab to account for failing to follow 'The LORD God of Israel'. Elijah steps forward when God calls him onto the scene.

King Ahab had turned away from God. I Kings 16:29-34 reports that Ahab *'did more evil in the eyes of the Lord than any of those before him'* (1 Kings 16:30). Ahab considered it trivial to continue in the sins of his father, King Jeroboam. He married Jezebel, a none Israelite, and began to worship her god, Baal, a fertility god, 'Lord of Rain and Dew'. Ahab also rebuilt Jericho in direct disobedience to the prophetic curse pronounced by Joshua against the one who would rebuild Jericho (Joshua 6:26). On rebuilding Jericho, Ahab's first and youngest sons died because he disobeyed God (1 Kings 16:34).

A seemingly anonymous Elijah came onto the scene to confront the sin of Ahab and Baal. He announced, *'As the LORD, the God of Israel, lives, whom I serve, there will neither be dew nor rain in the next few years except at my word'* (1 King 17:1). The battle lines were not only drawn up between Ahab and Elijah but, more importantly, between Baal, the Lord of Rain and Dew, and the LORD God of Israel, creator of heaven and earth. Elijah announces God's punishment for worshipping Baal to be in the form of a drought, a direct challenge as to who really is in control of rain and dew! The conflict between religious allegiances in Israel was a battle between God and the spiritual powers of Baal. Paul's teaching in Ephesians 6:12 is apt, *'For our struggle is not against flesh and blood, but against the authorities, against the rulers, against the powers of this dark world and against the spiritual forces of evil in the heavenly realms.'*

Elijah experienced God's protection and provision. Having confronted Ahab, God tells Elijah to hide. Elijah was provided with water from the brook in Kerith Ravine and fed by ravens (I Kings 17:2-6). When, during the drought, the brook dried up, God directed Elijah to a widow in Zarephath to supply him with food and water (1 Kings 17:9). The widow has water but has run out of flour and is concerned that her son will die of starvation. The account reveals the miraculous provision of flour for bread until the drought ends (1 Kings 17:14-16). Having saved the boy's life once by the provision of flour, when he dies of illness, the boy is raised back to life as Elijah prays for him. *'Then he (Elijah) cried out to the LORD, "LORD my God, have you brought tragedy to this widow I am staying with by causing her son to die?" Then he stretched himself out on the boy three times and cried out to the LORD, "LORD my God, let this boy's life return to him."* God heard and answered the prayer, and *'the boy's life returned to him!'* (1 Kings 17:19-21).

I am aware that at the time of writing, many people are experiencing hunger through grain shortages resulting from the war in Ukraine, climate change and cost of living increases. Prayer and action in caring for those in desperate need are on the agenda of churches and relief organisations. Food banks, zero food waste schemes, debt counselling and lobbying parliament, are some of the ways prayer leads us into action. As we pray, we are encouraged by examples of God's past provision, which spurs us on in our ministry and mission and become vehicles of God's provision to others.

For Reflection...

1.1. Which Bible story speaks to you most powerfully of God's provision?

1.2. In your praying, what is the balance between praying about your own needs and praying about the needs of others?

1.3. What action does the Lord want you to take to help provide for those in great need?

I Kings 18 is in the third year of the drought. Elijah received the word of the LORD to go to meet Ahab with the promise, *'I will send rain'* (1 Kings 18:2). Ahab, recognising that the famine is severe, sends Obadiah, the palace administrator, to look for any sources of water in the land. During the drought, Obadiah, a follower of God, was protecting the prophets, hiding them in caves, and supplying them with water and food (1 Kings 18:4). While searching for water, Obadiah meets Elijah, who asks Obadiah to convey a message to Ahab, *'Elijah is here!'* (I Kings 18:8). Obadiah is reticent to do so. He fears that if he tells Ahab he has found Elijah, the Spirit of the Lord will take Elijah away again. Obadiah recounts his faithfulness to God and his fear that Ahab would kill him if Elijah did not go to Ahab. Elijah allayed Obadiah's fear with the reassurance, *'As the LORD Almighty lives, whom I serve, I will surely present myself to Ahab today'* (1 Kings 18:15).

I Kings 18:16-45 is the account of God's victory over the Baals. Elijah meets Ahab, who labels him Israel's troublemaker (1 Kings 18:17). Elijah responds that Ahab is the source of Israel's trouble through disobeying God and following the Baals. How often is the one who obeys God branded the troublemaker by those who are disobedient to God?

A power confrontation then occurs between the 450 prophets of Baal and Elijah. Elijah makes a challenge. First, the prophets of Baal are to go and prepare a bull for burnt sacrifice. They are to call down fire from Baal. Elijah will then do the same, calling down fire from God. The challenge is, *'The god who answers by fire – he is God'* (1 Kings 18:24).

The 450 prophets call upon their Baal for several hours with no response. Elijah taunts them to shout louder in case he is deep in thought, or busy, or travelling, or asleep (I Kings 18:27). The prophets enter into a frenzy, cutting themselves, following their customs. There was no response. No fire came to light the sacrifice.

It is then Elijah's turn. He prepared an altar of twelve stones representing the twelve tribes of Jacob. He then dug a trench around it. He prepared the bull for sacrifice and invited the prophets of Baal to pour four large jars of water over the bull and the wood. At the time of the (daily) sacrifice, Elijah prayed, asking the LORD to prove he was God of Israel by sending fire and turning the people's hearts back to him. In response, *'Then the fire of the LORD fell and burned up the sacrifice, the wood, the stones and the soil, and also licked up the water in the trench'* (I Kings 18:38). The people responded, *'The LORD – he is God! The LORD – he is God'* (1

Kings 18:39). Elijah had faith in God. In response to his faith, God won the hearts of his people by answering with fire.

Elijah ordered the death of the 450 prophets. The wrath of God against sin, exercised by Elijah, is difficult for us to understand. A cancer surgeon, in a Local Preachers' Conference I led, called this act the equivalent of him removing all traces of cancer in a patient. He would not want traces to remain, causing cancer to spread again. This act removed the temptation to return to worshipping Baal. Such an act was not hurried or without the opportunity for repentance. The people had three years to return to God during the drought.

We then have the account of Elijah praying for the rain to come. Seven times he returned to prayer until a cloud appeared and heavy rain started falling. In the letter of James 5: 17-18, Elijah's prayer for rain is an example of persistent prayer, *'The prayer of a righteous person is powerful and effective'* (James 5:16). Elijah had received the promise that God would send rain (1 Kings 18:1). He exercised faith in believing God would answer with fire in the challenge to the prophets of Baal. He then prayed the promise that the rain would come. Six times, he sent his servant to look for signs of a cloud as a sign of the coming rain. *'There is nothing there,'* was the reply (1 Kings 18:43). On the seventh time of asking, Elijah's servant saw a small cloud begin to form. Soon after, heavy rain then began to fall (1 Kings 18:45). The LORD God, rather than Baal, controls the rain and the dew. Elijah, despite there being no sign of rain on six occasions, continued to trust God would be true to his promise. On the seventh time, there was a sign of the answer. Elijah, as James later reflected, is an example of persistent prayer. In the Sermon on Mount, Jesus said, *'Ask and it will be given to you; seek and you will find; knock and the door will be opened to you. For everyone who asks receives; the one who seeks finds; and to the one who knocks, the door will be opened'* (Matthew 7:7-8). The

Amplified Version captures the present continuous form of the Greek verbs, emphasising the encouragement of persistent prayer and the promise of receiving God's answer. *'Ask and keep on asking and it will be given to you; seek and keep on seeking and you will find; knock and keep on knocking and the door will be opened to you. For everyone who keeps on asking receives, and he who keeps on seeking finds, and to him who keeps on knocking, it will be opened'* (Matthew 7:7-8 Amplified Version).

We have gained a picture of Elijah being an ordinary man with an extraordinary ministry. He experienced the provision and protection of God. He saw the miraculous and won a great victory on Mount Carmel. Surely Elijah would remain strong in the Lord, having experienced answers to his prayers and faithfulness?

Using one of the timelines described in the introduction, we could plot a steep decline in his physical, mental, emotional and spiritual state in 1 Kings 19. As we read the story, we discover he was physically tired, mentally depressed, emotionally drained and spiritually empty. Elijah received a death threat from Jezebel, Ahab's wife. *'May the gods deal with me, be it ever so severely, if by this time tomorrow I do not make your life like that of one of them (the prophets of Baal). Elijah was afraid and ran for his life'* (1 Kings 19:2-3).

Elijah's sudden change of heart could be described as burn out or depression. From the mountain top experience, he plummeted into the depths. Elijah went into the wilderness and prayed, *'I have had enough, LORD. Take my life; I am no better than my ancestors'* (I Kings 19:4). He was undoubtedly honest with God. He was at the end of the line. The process of renewal began with God meeting his physical needs. Having prayed, Elijah lay down and slept. Later, an angel woke him and told him to eat, providing bread and water. Elijah then slept again. A second time the angel woke him and fed him to strengthen him for the journey. He then travelled 40 days and forty nights until he reached Mount Horeb, also known as Mount Sinai.

When we are feeling down after a stressful time, we need to take time to recover. Jesus made this clear to his disciples. On their return from their first independent mission trip, Jesus said, *'Come with me by yourselves to a quiet place and get some rest'* (Mark 6:31). Elijah certainly qualified for some rest and recovery. So do you and I. When we have been through a busy, stressful time and we feel overwhelmed by work, family needs or the needs of the world, we need to take time out to rest and recover. Again Jesus says, *'Come to me, all you who are weak and burdened, and I will give you rest'* (Matthew 11:28). It is worth remembering that we are human beings rather than human doings. We need our sabbath rest. I enjoy walking beside rivers or the sea. Liverpool Otterspool Promenade or the local parks are places where I experience renewal. We need time to receive from Jesus, taking time out from rushing around serving him (Luke 10:38-42).

For Reflection...

1.4. In what ways have times of being in the wilderness enriched your Christian life?

1.5. Are there any particular places that have helped your spiritual formation? And if so, what was it that actually helped?

1.6. What environments/places help you to experience God's renewing presence?

1.7. If you are not easily able to get out and about, how could you make somewhere within your home a space to rest and be renewed?

Elijah is an example of someone whose time of renewal began with rest and food. A forty-day walk in the wilderness may not seem to bring rest or relaxation. The wilderness is often used as a metaphor to suggest periods of spiritual dryness. It is a place of wandering or desolation. It is also a place of spiritual formation. Jesus' forty days in the wilderness clarified his mission. He experienced the tests offering a pathway to provide for his needs, protect him from harm and receive public acclaim and worship (Matthew 4:1-11). Instead, Jesus chose the path of humility, service and death, laying aside his equality with God, until that day when every knee will bow before him and proclaim him Lord (Philippians 2:5-11).

Wilderness is often a place of spiritual formation. God caught Moses' attention in the wilderness, speaking from the burning bush (Exodus 3). The 40 years of wandering in the wilderness were not only a time of correction for the Hebrews but of spiritual formation. The period in exile was a time of correction and formation of Jewish identity and faith in God. God's mystery and majesty surprised Ezekiel, *'by the Kebar River in the land of the Babylonians'* (Ezekiel 1:3). The wilderness is not a place where God is absent but where God often comes and takes us through the next stage of spiritual formation.

God took Elijah on such a journey to Mount Horeb, also known as Mount Sinai, the place of Moses' encounter with God. God enquired, *'What are you doing here, Elijah?'* (1 Kings 19:9b). Elijah presents his credentials to God, *'I have been very zealous for the LORD God Almighty.'* Elijah recalls the spiritual state of the nation, *'The Israelites have rejected your covenant, torn down your altars, and put your prophets to death with the sword.'* Elijah reveals his current state, *'I am the only one left, and now they are trying to kill me too.'* (1 Kings 19:10). Elijah is being honest with God.

A friend of mine wears a t-shirt with a shoal of fish swimming in the same direction. In the middle of the shoal, one fish is swimming in the opposite direction. Elijah felt that way. Perhaps you and I think that too. Being a Christian may go against the tide of family opinion, let alone public opinion. The sense of isolation may be overwhelming.

It is in the moment of isolation, depression and desolation that God instructs Elijah to stand on the mountain as *'the LORD is about to pass by'* (1 Kings 19:11). God invited Elijah to experience his presence. It is worth comparing the experiences of Moses and Elijah on Mount Sinai. Moses encountered the presence of God on Mount Sinai with thunder and lightning, a cloud, a trumpet blast, fire and smoke, the mountain trembled (earthquake), and finally, the voice of God (Exodus 19:16-19). The footnote to verse 19 in the NIV says, *'and God answered him with thunder.'* The NRSV says, *'Moses would speak and God would answer in thunder'* (Exodus 19: 19). An awesome, dramatic experience, signs of God's presence. Elijah experienced wind, an earthquake, fire and a gentle whisper (1 Kings 19:11-13). The same but different. A power encounter with the awesome God, speaking not with thunder but a gentle whisper. Elijah responded by standing at the cave entrance where he had been hiding (1 Kings 19:9, 13).

I remember the Revd Malcolm Sharrock, in the 1980s teaching on the outpouring of the Holy Spirit. One outpouring of the Holy Spirit happened at Pentecost with wind and fire, tongues, witnesses, preaching, and thousands coming to faith (Acts 2). The other on Easter Evening, when Jesus said, *'"Peace be with you! As the Father has sent me, I am sending you." And with that he breathed on them and said, "Receive the Holy Spirit"'* (John 20:21-22). What a contrast. Do we look for the powerful experience or the peaceful breath of the Holy Spirit? I have shared that teaching on countless occasions. One minister in tears explained how he had always desired the dramatic experience of the touch of the Holy Spirit. He now recognised he had experienced the gentle, peaceful breath of the Holy Spirit. A time for healing for him and several others. Perhaps for you too.

Moses needed the powerful voice, Elijah the gentle whisper.

Again, the LORD asked Elijah, *'What are you doing here?'* Elijah repeats his earlier response (1 Kings 19:13- 14).

God then redirects Elijah's life and thinking. He is told to, *'Go back the way you came.'* He received a new calling. He is to anoint two kings, Hazael over Aram, and Jehu the son of Nimshi over Israel. He is to anoint Elisha as his successor. There will be a judgement upon the nation. The culmination of the renewed calling is the affirmation that Elijah is not alone. God assures him saying, *'Yet I reserve seven thousand in Israel – all whose knees have not bowed down to Baal and whose mouths have not kissed him'* (1 Kings 19:18).

Perhaps the words, 'You are not alone,' are words you need to hear as you seek to be faithful to God. It is the affirmation and pick-me-up you need to return to a closer walk with God. It may be an opportunity to mentor a young Christian or family member, as Elijah did in mentoring his successor Elisha. It may be in your workplace, where you are a godly influence. It may be in your church fellowship, playing your part in serving the community of faith and the community the church serves.

We may not rise to the heights of Elijah, but the renewal he received is a renewal we can receive through the Holy Spirit. The 'still small voice of calm' leads us on until we see or enter the Kingdom of Heaven, and like Elijah, fellowship with Jesus (Mark 9:2-13).

For Reflection...

1.8. In what ways has experiencing God's great power helped your Christian journey?

1.9. In what ways has experiencing God's gentle presence helped your Christian journey?

1.10. Bring to the Lord any aspects of your life where you need his renewal, and be open for his response...

2: Are You Thirsty?

'Let anyone who is thirsty come to me and drink.'

John 7:37

In our previous study, we saw that the LORD, rather than Baal, was the giver of water. The LORD withheld water from the land for three years as a judgement on the people forsaking him. The battle on Mount Carmel saw the LORD setting fire to the water-soaked sacrifice on the altar. The drought came to an end, fulfilling the promise of God. The burnt-out Elijah received water and food for the journey to Mount Horeb, where he experienced spiritual renewal in the gentle whisper.

God's people ought to have known better. During the Exodus, as the people travelled through the wilderness, they complained to Moses that there was no water. They quarrelled and said, 'Give us water to drink' (Exodus 17 2). Moses did not see this as merely a complaint against him. The people were testing God (Exodus 17:3). God had already provided food for them in the wilderness through manna and quail (Exodus 16). However, the people were concerned for themselves and their livestock, who might die of thirst. The people threatened to stone Moses, who cried out to God for help. God heard Moses' request and gave him directions. He was to take his staff, which he had used to strike the Nile for the various plagues in Egypt and strike a rock on Horeb. 'I will stand before you by the rock of Horeb. Strike the rock, and water will come out of it for the people to drink. So Moses did this in the sight of the elders of Israel' (Exodus 17:6). The water flowed. Moses called the place Massah (testing) and Meribah (quarrelling), 'Because the Israelites quarrelled and because they tested the LORD saying, "Is the LORD among us or not?"' (Exodus 17:7).

Later in the Exodus, the people again quarrelled about a lack of water (Number 20: 1-13). On this occasion, God told Moses to take Aaron and his staff and, 'Speak to that rock before their *eyes and it will pour out its water. You will bring water out for the rock for the community so they and their livestock can drink'* (Numbers 20:8). Moses, however, was angry with the people. In his anger, instead of speaking to the rock, he struck the rock twice with his staff. Water gushed out. However, the LORD rebuked Moses. *'Because you did not trust in me enough to honour me as holy in the sight of the Israelites, you will not bring this community into the land I give them'* (Numbers 20:12). This place was also called Meribah, a place of quarrelling.

It is interesting that although the LORD had shown he had control over water, separating the Nile and bringing water from the rock, they followed Baal, the Lord of rain and dew, instead of the LORD, creator of heaven and earth. The Israelites were very forgetful of all God did for them. One of God's names in the Old Testament is Jehovah-Jireh, the God who provides. The Israelites, in difficult times, forgot that God, who provided in the past, could provide for their present needs. The Israelites are not alone. We do that all the time.

Equally, Moses reveals a lesson that God might provide from the same source but by different means. On the second occasion, in his anger, Moses struck the rock rather than spoke to the rock. A gracious God still provided water, but Moses did not set foot in the Promised Land.

My grandparents were members of the Salvation Army. At my infant baptism, they gave me a Bible with the verse, *'But my God shall supply all your need according to his riches in glory by Christ Jesus.'* (Philippians 4:19 AV). It was a word of blessing upon a 6-week-old grandson based on their experience of life. I have found that verse to be true from childhood to now. It does not mean that I don't doubt or get frustrated at times, but that verse and reflecting on God's provision encourages me to keep trusting that God is faithful.

One of the ways that the Israelites were to remember God's provision in the wilderness was through celebrating various festivals. In Leviticus 23:33-44, God instigates the Festival of Tabernacles. The Festival of Tabernacles lasts seven days, plus a sacred festival on the eighth day, remembering God's provision from Egypt through the wilderness into the Promised Land. During the Festival, they are to build and live in shelters made from palm, willow and other leafy trees. It is an occasion to rejoice in God's provision, not only in the past but in the present. It was a harvest festival, taking place in October once the crops had been gathered. After the exile, Ezra read about the Festival of Tabernacles, which was then reinstated and celebrated by the people (Nehemiah 8:13-18).

In John 7:14-10:21, Jesus attends and teaches at the Festival of Tabernacles. At this stage of its development, the Festival was a harvest festival celebrating God's provision during the forty years in the wilderness. It also looked forward to the outpouring of the Holy Spirit in the last days. Each morning of the Festival, the High Priest led a procession to the pool of Siloam, where he filled a golden flagon with water. He then led the procession back through the Water Gate to the temple. The people gathered to watch the procession, singing Psalms. At the sound of the three blasts from the Sofar (trumpet), they waved branches and shouted three times, 'Give thanks to the Lord.' At the temple, the High Priest took the water and daily wine offering and poured them into their respective silver bowls before placing them on the altar as a drink offering to the LORD. The two ceremonies related to the LORD's provision of water in the desert and looked forward to the outpouring of the Holy Spirit in the last days (D. Carson, The Gospel According to John, Pillar New Testament Commentary, Grand Rapids, MI: Eerdmans, ISBN 0-851-11749-X, p322-3).

Jesus initially stayed away from the Festival of Tabernacles as the Jewish leaders *'were looking to kill him'* (John 7:1). His brothers, however, encouraged him to go to increase his status as a public figure. The Jewish leaders hated him because Jesus challenged their teaching and confronted evil. Aware of their plot against him, Jesus delayed going to the Festival, choosing to go secretly rather than as a public figure and began to teach *'halfway through the festival'* (John 7:14). People responded differently to Jesus. For some, he was a good man. To others, he was a great deceiver of the people. The Jewish leaders objected to Jesus healing a boy on the sabbath, as this broke the Sabbath Law (John 7:16-35). Jesus argued that he was doing no more than healing the whole of the boy. If the leaders could circumcise on the sabbath when there was a conflict between the law of circumcision on the eighth day and the Sabbath Law, then Jesus could also heal on the sabbath. The crowd affirmed Jesus' thinking that the authorities were trying to kill him (John 7:6 cf 7:25).

Another area of conflict was a question of authority. By what power and authority did Jesus heal and teach? Jesus was not under the control of the religious leaders. Jesus responded that he was subject to the authority of God who had sent him (John 7:28). Many believed in Jesus. Others were ready to kill him. Jesus then hinted about his death and resurrection. *'Jesus said, "I am with you for only a short time, and then I am going to the one who sent me. You will look for me; and where I am, you cannot come"'* (John 7:33-34).

The next block of teaching is in the context of the Festival, emphasising the morning sacrifice of a drink offering of water and wine, representing God's provision for life and the coming Holy Spirit.

> 'On the last and greatest day of the festival, Jesus stood and said in a loud voice, "Let anyone who is thirsty come to me and drink. Whoever believes in me, as Scripture has said, rivers of living water will flow from within them." By this he meant the Spirit, whom those who believed in him were later to receive. Up to that time the Spirit had not been given, since Jesus had not yet been glorified' (John 7:37-39).

There are two schools of thought on which day of the Festival Jesus said this; day seven or eight? Which day was the 'last and greatest day of the festival'? Leviticus said that that festival lasted seven days, with the eighth a sabbath rest. The seventh day was the last day when the water procession took place, and the water was part of the drink offering to God. At the time of Jesus, the Jews may have regarded day eight as 'the greatest day of the festival.' It was a day of rejoicing and thanksgiving. Whichever day you choose, when Jesus shouted that all who were thirsty could come to him, he was making the point that he was the source of life-giving water. John, in an editorial note, noted that this referred to the outpouring of the Holy Spirit following Jesus' death and resurrection. Both water and Holy Spirit were crucial to the meaning of the Festival. Both elements found their fulfilment in Jesus.

As we unpack this teaching, we note that the invitation is open to all. 'Let anyone who is thirsty.' Thirst is an experience common to everyone. Physically, we need clean water to drink as men are 60% water and women 55% water. As water is lost, so we become thirsty and need to have water replaced. That was the physical condition remembered in the Festival of Tabernacles. During the Exodus, the people were thirsty, and God met their needs from the rock.

The New Testament uses the metaphor of Jesus as the rock in several ways.

- Jesus' teaching is the rock on which we must build our lives, giving stability and security through the storms of life (Matthew 7: 24-27).
- Jesus is the stone the builders rejected (Matthew 21:42 and Psalm 118:22-23). As we have seen in John 7, Jesus is a stumbling block for many people. Some accepted his ministry, while others rejected his ministry and still do.
- Jesus is the church's cornerstone (Matthew 21:42 and Psalm 118:22-23). A building's cornerstone provides a reference point for the correctness of the vertical and horizontal lines of the walls. As the church's cornerstone, Jesus defines what is right and wrong in doctrine and practice. We measure our love and knowledge of God and the love and service of others against the example and teaching of Jesus. The title of Jesus as the cornerstone and Psalm 118:22-23 is quoted several times in the New Testament (Acts 4:11, 1 Peter 2:6-7).
- Jesus is the rock from which water flows. Paul, in 1 Corinthians 10:1-5, warns the Corinthians about disobedience to God's teaching. In particular, he refers to the provision of God during the Exodus. God provided manna and water, spiritual food and drink. Paul adds, *'for they drank from the spiritual rock that accompanied them, and that rock was Christ'* (1 Corinthians 10:4). Seeing Jesus as the source of living water, he draws the link with Christ, the rock, the water source in the wilderness. Is this linked to Jesus' teaching at the Festival of the Tabernacles? Is it connected to Jesus' opening their minds so they could understand the Scriptures, meaning the Law of Moses, the Prophets, and the Psalms? (Luke 24:27, Luke 24:44-45) Paul saw the pre-incarnate Jesus as the rock, the water source in the wilderness.

In the Old Testament, thirst is both a physical and a spiritual condition. Psalm 42 begins, *'As the deer pants for the streams of water, so my soul pants for you, my God. My soul thirst for God, for the living God. When can I go and meet God?'* The image is of a deer whose every sinew is crying out for water in an arid land. The psalmist recognises that the thirst for God is similar. It is a cry of desperation. It has a faint echo of the people in the wilderness, *'I say to God my Rock, "Why have you forgotten me?" ..... My enemies taunt me, saying to me all day long, "Where is your God"'* (Psalm 42:9). The answer for the psalmist is to put his hope in God, *'for I will yet praise him, my Saviour and my God'* (Psalm 42:11).

To all those crying out, even wondering whether God has forgotten or forsaken them, Jesus shouts, *'Let anyone who is thirsty come to me.'* There is a mission imperative for each church and Christian. We know the source of life-giving water or life in all its fullness (John 7:37 cf. John 10:10). Our task is to point people to Jesus, our Saviour, provider, peace, and healer.

For Reflection...

2.4. Have there been times in your life when you have felt forsaken by God? If so, what helped you through such difficult times?

2.5. In what ways have other Christians helped you to discover that you have not been forsaken by God?

2.6. Which Bible verses reassure you that God is close enough to help you through?

During the Covid-19 lockdown, people were praying and seeking the comfort of God, even attending our Zoom and online services. In their need, people sought God through the church for comfort and strength. People had the technical savvy to find churches online, telephone services, receive printed services through their doors or phone friends and neighbours for support and prayer. Sadly, in many places, the early hope has not translated into continuing links or growth in the reach of churches.

During the war in Ukraine, we have observed a nation at prayer. As their worldwide family, we have joined in praying for peace. The BBC news on 22 June 2022 followed a charity bringing people to safety from cities under attack. The news reporter commented that before starting the journey, the team prayed for safety and protection. The report stated that a bomb had exploded on the road a few hundred yards ahead of the convoy. The reporter noted that if the group had not stopped to pray, the bomb would have hit the convoy. The team were then able to bring people to safety.

The church's calling is to offer Jesus to those in physical, emotional, mental or spiritual need. In our preaching, prayers, and service, we present Jesus. The same Holy Spirit who anointed Jesus dwells in us, *'to proclaim good news to the poor, proclaim freedom for the prisoners, recovery of sight to the blind, to set the oppressed free, to proclaim the year of the Lord's favour'* (Luke 4:18-19). We offer Jesus in a busy marketplace. Yet we must raise our voices above the cacophony of noise and loudly declare Jesus' invitation, *'Let anyone who is thirsty come to me and drink.'*

Jesus then makes the promise to the hearers, which he had made individually to the woman at the well in John 4, *'Everyone who drinks this water will be thirsty again, but whoever drinks the water I give them will never thirst. Indeed, the water I give them will become in them a spring welling up to eternal life'* (John 4:13-14). The woman who needed more than physical water received spiritual affirmation from the man, *'who told me everything I ever did'* (John 4:29). Jesus met her where she was. He took her spiritual conversation seriously. He addressed her deep need and the reality of her situation. He connected with her, and she and the whole village were changed. Here we have a pattern of talking about God. By attentive listening and sensitive response, we can address a person's need, even leading to faith. To the thirsty, Jesus offers a spring welling up to eternal life.

The water offered by Jesus at the Festival of Tabernacles results from believing in Jesus. Jesus has evoked a mixed response in the festival worshippers. For some, he is good, the Messiah and from God. For others, he is the deceiver. Some may be followers. Others wanted to seize him and kill him.

Jesus encourages the crowd to believe who he is by what he has done. However, the most significant faith builder will be in accepting Jesus' death and resurrection. For John, the events of Good Friday and Easter Day glorify Jesus (John 7:39). It is the cornerstone for some but the scandal and stumbling block for others.

At this point, we need to decide who Jesus is for us. Is Jesus the cornerstone of our life or the stumbling block? Is Jesus our Lord and Saviour offering forgiveness, and healing our relationship with God? Does Jesus change God from being a judge to a gracious Father receiving us into his family? Is our heart strangely warmed, and with John Wesley, we know that we are a child of God?

For Reflection...

2.7. Who is Jesus to you? Spend a few moments carefully considering each of the questions in the paragraph above...

2.8. How does God see you? Look at those same questions, and consider how God's sees you. Does he see that Jesus is your cornerstone, Lord and Saviour? Is the gracious Father saying that you are his child?

In his Gospel's editorial note, John helps us understand what the rivers of living water are that will flow within those who come to Jesus. The note says, 'By this he meant the Holy Spirit, whom those who would believe in him were later to receive. Up to that time, the Spirit had not been given, since Jesus had not been glorified' (John 7:39). In this comment, the Holy Spirit is not an abstract spirit but a person. The Holy Spirit is the 'whom' that people would receive.

In John's Gospel, the disciples received the Holy Spirit as the risen Jesus breathed on them. On Easter Sunday evening, as they gathered behind the locked doors, Jesus offered them peace and forgiveness, breathed on them and said, 'Receive the Holy Spirit' (John 20:22). Imagine how terrified the disciples must have been. They were behind locked doors for fear of the Jewish leaders. They were scared for their lives. The disciples must have been anxious about how Jesus would respond to their actions on and after his arrest. They scattered at his arrest. Peter denied Jesus three times. John seems to have been the only one who followed Jesus, watched his trial and was present at Jesus' crucifixion. However, Jesus allayed their fears with the word of peace. Peace (shalom) speaks of peace between people, inner peace, and peace with God and creation. At that moment, Jesus renewed their relationship with him. They received inner peace for their failures. They experienced forgiveness.

The Holy Spirit is the gift to all who are thirsty. How do we receive such a gift?

From 2012 to 2018, I travelled throughout the mainland Districts of the Methodist Church of Britain as the development worker for Methodist Evangelicals Together. On one visit to the Scarborough circuit, my Sunday appointments were at a church with two morning services. My theme for both services was spiritual renewal. As the first service ended, one gentleman said, 'You spoke about the Holy Spirit but did not offer him to the congregation.'

I noticed that the gentleman was present for the second service. As I preached the same sermon, I recognised his words as a gentle rebuke from God. At the end of the service, I offered prayers for spiritual renewal for those who wished to come forward to receive a fresh anointing of the Holy Spirit. Many responded. After the service, I thanked the gentleman for his faithfulness in gently sharing God's word for me, and direction for my ministry. Over the next few years, as I travelled, I offered prayers for renewal at an appropriate time in the retreat or services I led. The numbers responding meant that I invited the local ministers or ministry teams to share in that ministry. I soon discovered that people were thirsty for God.

Often churches offer the opportunity for personal prayer after a service or at other times. If you are thirsty, those can be the opportunity to respond to Jesus' offer, *'Come to me and drink.'* As we come to Jesus, he keeps his promises, and we may find the gift of peace, love and joy filling our hearts. We may receive strength in all that we are facing. We may receive the gift of healing and wholeness. In response to our desire for our thirst to be quenched, Jesus *'Is able to do immeasurably more than all we ask or imagine according to his power that is at work within us'* (Ephesians 3:20).

However, we do not need to wait for such an opportunity. Even now, we can bring our thirst directly to God. Psalm 42 is the song of an individual or congregation thirsty for God's presence and touch. It is an honest Psalm. The worshipper admits to God how they are feeling. It speaks of thirst, not being able to or wanting to be in worship, downcast by life, and even forsaken by God. In the end, there is a resolute action, *'Put your hope in God, for yet I will praise him, my Saviour and my God'* (Psalm 42:11).

In expressing the hope that God will meet your needs and fill you with his Holy Spirit, pray the following:

Spirit of the living God,
Fall afresh on me;
Spirit of the living God,
Fall afresh on me.
Break me, melt me, mould me, fill me.
Spirit of the living God,
Fall afresh on me.

(Daniel Iverson)

For Reflection...

2.9. Thinking back over your Christian life, when have you been refreshed by the Holy Spirit?

2.10. On a regular basis, how can you be frequently refreshed?

2.11. In what ways can you invite others to come to Jesus and drink the living water of God's Spirit?

3: The Holy Spirit - The Helper

'And I will ask the Father, and he will give you another
advocate to help you and be with you for ever -
the Spirit of truth.'

John 14:16-17a

How many of us wish we had been a disciple during Jesus'
earthly ministry? We would have experienced Jesus' love and
compassion. We would have experienced Jesus' healing and
miracle-working ministry. We would have heard Jesus' teaching
to the crowds and personal conversations as he mentored the
disciples. We would have heard Jesus calling the religious
leaders to scriptural holiness rather than human tradition.
Having experienced all of this, we would have been shocked to
hear Jesus say, 'I am going away?' (John 14:28).

John chapters 13-17 are Jesus' farewell discourse to the
disciples. In these chapters, Jesus prepared his disciples for
life without him. Jesus recognises their mounting anxiety (John
14:1). He prepared them for his crucifixion and spoke of his
resurrection, though they did not understand what he was
saying. On hearing Jesus speaking this way, the disciples were
upset, bewildered, confused, and scared about the future.
Jesus was leaving them. What would happen to them?

In response, Jesus promised not to leave them alone. Jesus
promised to send them the Holy Spirit (John 14:15-31, 15:26-
16:15). The teaching explains how the Holy Spirit will fulfil the
roles of helper, teacher and evangelist. In this chapter, we will
unpack what this means.

Jesus' teaching speaks of the Holy Spirit not as a force but as a
person. The Holy Spirit is called alongside to help disciples
then and now. The Greek term is paraclete, a word unique to
John's writings in the New Testament. English versions of the
Bible translate paraclete in a variety of ways: Advocate (NRSV,

27

NIV 2011), Counsellor (NLT, NIV 1984), Helper (GNB, Tom Wright, NKJV, ESV), Comforter (LB), Friend (Message). In these translations, we have a richness of the one whom Jesus will send to quench our spiritual thirst and help us be disciples in the 21st century. Jesus' death, resurrection and ascension will not leave us as orphans but as cherished children of God.

If we return to the crucifixion of Jesus, Mark records, *'With a loud cry, Jesus breathed his last. The curtain of the temple was torn in two from top to bottom'* (Mark 15:37-38, also Matthew 27:50-51). The curtain mentioned is between the Holy Place and the Holy of Holies in the temple. The Ark of the Covenant, which contained the two tablets of the Ten Commandments given by God to Moses, was placed in the Holy of Holies. The top of the Ark was known as the mercy seat or atonement cover. Two golden cherubim, each with one wing outstretched and one wing touching each other, were above the Ark of the Covenant. Beneath the Cherubim's touching wings and above the mercy seat, God's presence dwelt. Each year, on the Day of Atonement, the High Priest entered through the curtain into the Holy of Holies. Before he could do so, he performed a sacrifice for the cleansing of his sins. On entering the Holy of Holies, he sprinkled the blood of the sacrifice on the mercy seat. The sacrifice cleansed the people of their sins. Instead of seeing the Law they had broken, God saw the sacrifice for the forgiveness of their sins. The blood of the sacrifice cleansed their sin, both as individuals and as a nation. At that moment, they were at one with God.

The letter to the Hebrews, chapters 5-10, explains Jesus' death in the context of the Day of Atonement. On his death, Jesus shed his blood for the forgiveness of sin. He entered into God's presence through the curtain, torn in two from top to bottom, from heaven to earth. That sacrifice made once and for all brought forgiveness, *'for all who obey him'* (Hebrews 5:9). Through Jesus' death, as we seek God's forgiveness, *'We have the confidence to enter the Most Holy Place'* (Hebrews 10:19-22).

Jesus' death opens the way for us into the presence of God, an intimacy of relationship, with the assurance that we are children of God.

The tearing of the curtain not only opens the way for us into God's presence. It also opens the way for God to enter us and make us the temple of the Holy Spirit. God, by His Holy Spirit, enters the disciples with peace and forgiveness on Easter evening (John 20:21-23). On the Day of Pentecost (Acts 2), the Holy Spirit filled them with power from God to continue the mission of Jesus of preaching, teaching, healing and deliverance (Matthew 4:23-25). God, the Holy Spirit, dwelt in people. Paul spoke of individuals and the fellowship of believers as the temple of the Holy Spirit (1 Corinthians 6:19, 3:16). At the Festival of Tabernacles, Jesus spoke of the Holy Spirit being rivers of living water flowing from within disciples. God, the Holy Spirit, dwells within us when we acknowledge Jesus as our Saviour. The Holy Spirit is alongside us to help and empower us for discipleship and mission.

For Reflection...

3.1 Thinking of the tearing of the curtain: What does it mean to you to be able to enter God's presence? In what ways have you benefitted by God's presence entering you?

3.2. Has the barrier of sin which prevents your oneness with God been removed? If 'No', it can be through repenting of your sin and trusting Jesus as your Saviour. If 'Yes', spend a few moments giving thanks for all that oneness with God means to you.

There are four paraclete sayings in John's Gospel:

- *'And I will ask the Father, and he will give you another advocate to help you and be with you forever - the Spirit of truth'* (John 14:16-17a)

- *'But the advocate, the Holy Spirit, whom the Father will send in my name, will teach you all things and will remind you of everything I have said to you'* (John 14:26)
- *'When the advocate comes, whom I will send to you from the Father - the Spirit of truth who goes out from the Father - he will testify about me'* (John 15:26-27)
- *'Unless I go away, the advocate will not come to you; but if I go, I will send him to you. When he comes, he will prove the world to be wrong about sin and righteousness and judgement: about sin, because people do not believe in me; about righteousness, because I am going to the Father, where you can see me no longer, and about judgement, because the prince of this world now stands condemned'* (John 16:7b-11)

In the contemporary literature to the New Testament, paraclete is used in several ways:

- Paraclete means called in to help or to render some service. The Holy Spirit is available to us to be our helper.
- Paraclete is also used to bring comfort and consolation in times of distress.
- Paraclete is the counsel for the defence, the one who bears witness to a person's character when under judgement. Jesus is the Paraclete in 1 John 2:1, *'My dear children, I write this to you so that you will not sin. But if anyone does sin, we have an advocate with the Father - Jesus Christ, the Righteous one.'* Jesus presents the case for our forgiveness, our acceptance of his death and the resurrection as the means of our salvation.
- Paraclete is used as the pep talk to urge people to noble deeds and high thoughts, the word of courage before the battle. In all that life throws at us, the Paraclete helps us to cope and conquer; it is none other than the power of the risen Christ.

The Holy Spirit does not work instead of or despite us, but in us and through us. The vitality of our Christian lives depends upon the Holy Spirit.

John 14:15-17, *'And I will ask the Father, and he will give you another advocate to help you and be with you forever - The Spirit of truth.'* The Greek word for *'another'* is *allos,* meaning 'another of the same kind' instead of 'another of a different kind.' Jesus would leave, but God the Father would send the Holy Spirit, who, like the Son of God, is present to help and comfort us. The Holy Spirit is the presence of the risen Jesus, *'I will not leave you as orphans; I will come to you'* (John 14:18).

The Holy Spirit as Helper

The Works of Jesus

I wonder, do you view the book of Acts as the acts of the apostles or the Holy Spirit? Similarly, do you consider the ministry of your church as the acts of the congregation or the Holy Spirit? Both then and now, the Holy Spirit anoints and empowers us to fulfil the ministry of Jesus in us and through us.

John 14:12 can be very contentious. *'Very truly I tell you, whoever believes in me will do the works I have been doing, and they will do even greater things than I have been doing, and they will even do greater things than these, because I am going to the Father.'* How can the disciples do works greater than Jesus? The works of Jesus are the preaching, teaching, healing and deliverance ministry. The Gospels give us plenty of examples. As John says, *'Jesus did many other things as well. If every one of them were written down, I suppose that even the whole world would not have room for the books that would be written'* (John 21:25).

Greater works are possible because after his finished work upon the cross, he rose again and ascended to the Father (John 16:10). Ten Days later, the Holy Spirit, sent by the Father, fills the disciples. The *'greater things'* over the next two millennia are the billions coming to faith, countless deeds of mercy and compassion, transformed lives, communities and nations, and miracles of healing and wholeness. These are works of Jesus by the power of the Holy Spirit, working through the body of Christ.

The Ministry of Prayer

The disciples' power to do greater things is rooted in prayer. Jesus promises, *'And I will do whatever you ask in my name, so that the Father may be glorified in the Son. You may ask me for anything in my name, and I will do it'* (John 14:13-14). We are not able to perform them: it is Christ in us who *'will do whatever we ask.'* 'In my name' is like adding, 'In Jesus' name,' at the end of a prayer. In Hebrew thought, the name expresses the essential character of the thing or person. To pray 'in Jesus' name' is to make a request entirely in harmony with Christ's character and His purposes. The Holy Spirit comes to our aid. He helps us to know what is God's will and purpose. He takes our moans and groans of the deep longings of our hearts and makes them known to the Father (Romans 8:26-27). The Holy Spirit helps us to know and pray the mind of Christ (1 Corinthians 2:16). When we pray in this way, we release the person and ministry of Jesus into our communities.

The Revelation of Truth

Throughout his earthly ministry, Jesus was on trial before the people. Like an advocate in a courtroom, he produced evidence and witnesses that he was sent from God and revealed the truth about God. The Holy Spirit, as paraclete, will pick up where Jesus left off. The Holy Spirit is called *'the Spirit of Truth'* (John 14:17; 15:26; 16:13). He would guide the apostles into truth and help them live out the truth. He would communicate the truth about God, revealed in Jesus (John 1:17; 4:24; 5:33; 8:32, 40). The incarnate Jesus was *'full of grace and truth'* (John 1:14). Jesus proclaimed himself to be *'The way, the truth and the life'* (John 14:6). The Holy Spirit continues, sustains, and affirms the truth of Jesus in each generation.

It is my daily prayer that the Holy Spirit will lead me into truth and enable me to convey that truth in all I say and do. The process begins with the Holy Spirit leading me into the truth about myself. He shows me my faults and failings but leads me to the cross, where the work of forgiveness and transformation takes place. He leads me into holiness. The great privilege of every believer is the indwelling of the Holy Spirit (John 7:38).

The Gift of Love

John declares, *'God is love'* (1 John 4:8). The Holy Spirit, the third person of the Trinity, brings the eternal spring of God's love into our lives. Love is the first part of the nine-fold fruit of the Holy Spirit (Galatians 5:22) and the greatest gift (1 Corinthians 13:1). It is no wonder that Jesus expects the Holy Spirit to help us to obey his commands, *'Whoever has my commands and keeps them is the one who loves me'* (John 14:21,23,24). Obedience to Jesus' commands and teaching is the visible sign of our love for Jesus. We follow Jesus' commands, many of which we find very hard and contrary to our nature, not out of legalism or fear of punishment but out of love for him. The Old Testament is the narrative of a people struggling to obey God. Yet God does not give up on them. There is the promise of a new heart, the gift of the Holy Spirit, to enable the people to obey God's laws (Ezekiel 36:26-27). As we grow in our discipleship, love for God grows daily.

Richard of Chichester offers us the following prayer,

Thanks be to thee, my Lord Jesus Christ,
for all the benefits thou hast given me,
for all the pains and insults thou hast borne for me.
O most merciful redeemer, friend and brother,
may I know thee more clearly,
love thee more dearly,
and follow thee more nearly, day by day.
Amen.

The Gift of Peace

We have already addressed the gift of peace given to the disciples on Easter Day evening as he breathed the Holy Spirit upon the disciples. Jesus promised this as a parting gift for the disciples. *'Peace I leave with you; my peace I give you. I do not give to you as the world gives. Do not let your hearts be troubled and do not let them be afraid'* (John 14:27).

In New Testament times the normal way to say good-bye was peace (šālôm). In his death Jesus provided a legacy for His disciples: My peace I give you. They would have *'peace with God'* (Romans 5:1) because their sins were forgiven and the *'peace of God'* (Philippians 4:7) would guard their lives. Jesus' shalom brings an end to the brokenness and separation caused by sin. Nothing in the world can offer such a gift. The world's false peace comes from blinding us to our peril or blinding us with our pride. It's unable to give this shalom kind of peace that allows us to face the stark realities of life in calm assurance. Even the fear of death (Hebrews 2:14-15) and fear of the future are removed as Jesus' followers trust in him and live in the fruit of the Spirit (John 20:19-26). Thus they need not be troubled (John 14:1).

The peace which the Holy Spirit offers is not merely the lack of conflict but peace during the conflict. Paul describes this as, *'The peace of God, which transcends all understanding, will guard your hearts and minds in Christ Jesus'* (Philippians 4:7). The idea behind this verse is that we are in the 'fortress' of Christ Jesus. Whatever is going in or around us, we know ourselves to be safe in his love. Such peace is beyond human understanding but is a fruit of the Holy Spirit's work in our lives. I am a natural worrier. On occasions, I am anxious and fearful (especially at night). However, I know that whatever is happening, I am safe in God's love. If, like me, you have bouts of anxiety, allow the Holy Spirit to fill you with Christ's peace (Philippians. 4:6-7).

The Gift of Praise

Jesus prophesied his departure and the coming of the Spirit to encourage the disciples' faith, *'Now I have told you before it happens, so that when it happens, you may believe'* (John 14:29).

Fulfilled prophecy is a great comfort and support to believers. Jesus had predicted his death and resurrection many times (Mark 8:31-32; 9:31, 10:32-34). Jesus would be obedient to the Father's purposes no matter what it might cost him personally. When Jesus' suffering and death came to pass, it would shake the disciples' faith. Through Easter Saturday, they must have been grieving, and I wonder if any remembered Jesus' promise of resurrection. The resurrection on Easter Day fulfilled his promise. From that moment on, they trusted the promises of Jesus. 'They will trust their Master all the more when they see his words verified' (Leon Morris, Gospel According to John, The New International Commentary, 1971, p 659). The promised resurrection can assure us that Jesus will be faithful in all he promises.

For Reflection...

3.3. How can Christians today do 'even greater things than' than Jesus did during his earthly ministry? (John 14:14)

3.4. During your Christian life, what have been the most valuable ways in which you have experienced the Holy Spirit helping you?

3.5. In what areas of your life and ministry do you need more help from the Holy Spirit?

The Holy Spirit as Evangelist

Our son, Matthew, was a professional dancer. On one occasion, we went to a production in which he was dancing. To our surprise, he was the male lead in Lord of the Dance. When he was on stage, the spotlight was upon him. The lighting team focussed the audience's attention upon him. They had a key role, but not to draw attention to themselves.

The work of the Holy Spirit in evangelism focuses on the person and ministry of Jesus. His work is also to equip disciples of every generation for this work.

Jesus said, *'When the Advocate comes, whom I will send you from the Father - the Spirit of truth who goes out from the Father – he will testify about me. And you also must testify, for you have been with me from the beginning'* (John 15:26-27). After Jesus' return to the Father, there must be a continuing witness to Jesus. We tend to focus on the last part of the verse, *'And you also must testify.'* While it refers to the first disciples, we recognise the ongoing work of witnessing about Jesus is ours. The good news is that we have the Holy Spirit to help us.

In John's Gospel, he lists seven witnesses to Jesus' character and power.

1. Jesus' witness about himself (5:31)
2. John the Baptist (5:33)
3. The Works of Jesus (5:36)
4. The Father (5:37-38)
5. The Scriptures (5:39-40)
6. The Holy Spirit (15:26)
7. The Disciples (15:27)

We see from that list that in the debate on the authority of Jesus to perform healing on the sabbath, Jesus referred to five witnesses. In the Final Discourse, Jesus introduces the witness of the Holy Spirit and the disciples. The importance of the disciples is that they have been with Jesus and can testify about the teaching, preaching, healing and deliverance ministry of Jesus. They will be witnesses of his death and resurrection. John begins his first letter with the affirmation that the disciples proclaim all they have seen and heard and now share the gospel of eternal life (1 John 1:1-4).

In John 16:7-11, Jesus outlines the Holy Spirit's work as the evangelist.

> 'Unless I go away, the advocate will not come to you; but if I go, I will send him to you. When he comes, he will prove the world to be wrong about sin and righteousness and judgement: about sin, because people do not believe in me; about righteousness, because I am going to the Father, where you can see me no longer, and about judgement, because the prince of this world now stands condemned.'

The first aspect of his evangelistic work is to *prove the world wrong about sin... about sin, because people do not believe in me'*. Some translations say, *'He will convict the world about sin.'* The word *elencho* behind the two translations carries the legal meaning of pronouncing the judicial verdict on the guilty. The Holy Spirit brings people to an understanding of how their lives fall short of God's standards. He then moves them to repentance. The Holy Spirit may take a conversation, a sermon, or the lifestyle and witness of Christians to show something is missing in their lives. A sense of searching begins, and the Holy Spirit points people to Jesus. Jesus and his life and ministry take on a new significance. The cross is a sign of God's love for them. Repentance, a changing direction to follow Jesus and his way of life, takes place. Peace, forgiveness, purpose and life in all its fullness are some ways people express the change in their lives.

The second aspect of the Holy Spirit's work in evangelism is to prove the righteousness of Jesus. Paul, in Ephesians 1:19b-20, comments on the power of the Holy Spirit available to the Christian. *'That power is the same as the mighty strength he exerted when he raised Jesus from the dead and seated him at the right hand in the heavenly realms.'* By the Holy Spirit raising Jesus from the dead, God proved Jesus' righteousness. *'The wages of sin is death'* (Romans 6:23). Jesus was raised from the dead because he was righteous before God, having never sinned. The Holy Spirit seeks to bring people to the knowledge of the forgiveness of sin and life eternal. As Jesus stated, *'I am the resurrection and the life. The one who believes in me will live, even though they die, and whoever lives, believing in me will never die. Do you believe this?'* (John 11:25). The invitation to eternal life is available through Jesus. The Holy Spirit can present the case. The hearer must answer the question, *'Do you believe this?'*

The final aspect of the Holy Spirit's work in evangelism is to prove people wrong about judgement and that the prince of the world now stands condemned. In the farewell discourse, Jesus says, *'I will not say much more to you, for the prince of this world is coming. He has no hold over me, but he comes so that the world may learn that I love the Father and do exactly what my Father has commanded'* (John 14:30-31). In obedience to the Father's will, rather than Satan's plans, Jesus will go to the cross. It is the place not of defeat for Jesus but victory. Jesus' death and resurrection have defeated sin and death.

All of the above is both a comfort and a challenge in evangelism and mission. It is a comfort to know the Holy Spirit is there to help us. It is a challenge that he shines a spotlight upon our lives and ministry to bring people to a knowledge and love for Jesus. It means that we are never off duty. We are the only Bible that people read. How we cope with life and all its ups and downs will take people along the pathway to faith. Our readiness to share our faith may be a significant step for a family member, friend or stranger. Christians are in every part of the community and society. We may gather for worship, but we disperse into communities. Our lives speak far more than our words. The Holy Spirit can use even you and me to take people on the road to faith. We need to make opportunities for people to explore faith through the various discipleship courses and discussion groups. Our daily prayer can be that God will use us to help people come to and grow in their Christian faith. Bill Hybels of the Willow Creek Community Church, Illinois, described evangelism in a very down-to-earth way. He said, 'Evangelism is not about crossing the sea or road, but crossing the road to tell a friend about your greatest friend.' Let us pray for such opportunities and ask the Holy Spirit to help us in that task.

The Holy Spirit as Teacher

The final paraclete saying is, *'But the advocate, the Holy Spirit, whom the Father will send in my name, will teach you all things and will remind you of everything I have said to you'* (John 14:26).

In South Chadderton Methodist Church, the church where I was nurtured in the Christian faith from a child until leaving University, I was encouraged to memorise Bible verses. Those verses in the Revised Standard Version often come to mind, providing help, assurance, comfort and thanksgiving. Equally, my daily Bible readings are relevant to everyday life. As things happen during the day, the Bible reading becomes appropriate and helpful. You may affirm similar occurrences in your life. They are all part of the process of being lifelong learners and growing in Christian discipleship.

It is the work of the Holy Spirit to teach and remind you of the teaching of Jesus. I pray for the Holy Spirit's help in understanding and explaining the Scriptures. The nearer Sunday gets, the more urgently I pray!

Jesus also hints at the prophetic ministry of the Holy Spirit. In John 16:12, Jesus recognises that his opportunity to teach the disciples is ending. The Holy Spirit will continue to guide them into all truth (John 16:13). Jesus uses the imagery of the Holy Spirit being part of the divine conversation with the Father and the Son and making that known to the disciples (John 16:13-

15). John, in his second and third letters, adds a note of caution to beware of false teachers and teaching, which can lead the church astray. We are to test that this teaching is consistent with the canon of Scripture, which is the rule of faith. We are to continue in the teaching of Jesus.

One of the gifts of being a Methodist minister is the circuit property steward. Especially as my DIY skills often mean Damage It Yourself! Other skilful people carry out what I can't do.

Returning to the start of the chapter, the disciples must have wondered how they could continue the ministry of Jesus on their own. Jesus assures them they do not need to be DIY disciples. The Holy Spirit will help and empower them to be Jesus' witnesses in Jerusalem, all Judea, Samaria and to the ends of the earth (Acts 1:8).

We have the same reassurance today. Even though we face tremendous challenges, the Holy Spirit will help us. We do not need to be DIY Christians. We need to receive and release the gift of the Holy Spirit in our lives. May the rivers of living water be released to quench the thirst and needs of our communities.

For Reflection...

3.6. If your religion is based on what you do for Jesus Christ, how can your reliance shift to what Jesus Christ has done for you?

3.7. In your service for Christ, how does your reliance on yourself compare with how much you are relying on the Holy Spirit?

3.8. How can you seek a greater awareness of the Holy Spirit alongside you?

4: Re-digging the Wells of Renewal

'Isaac reopened the wells that had been dug in the time of his Father Abraham.'

Genesis 26:18

In our Christian faith, there is a great danger that we can grow despondent because things are not what they used to be or are somewhere else. We remember large Junior Churches, higher attendances at worship, and times of spiritual renewal in our church and lives. If Jesus promised 'rivers of living water flowing from within us', why is there no evidence in our lives and churches? Perhaps it is time to take up our spiritual spades and reopen the wells of spiritual renewal. It is time to release the power of the Holy Spirit in our lives and churches.

John Wesley said the following in 1786.

> 'I am not afraid that the people called Methodists should ever cease to exist either in Europe or America. But I am afraid lest they should only exist as a dead sect, having the form of religion without the power. And this undoubtedly will be the case unless they hold fast both the doctrine, Spirit, and discipline with which they first set out.'

Those words are particularly relevant to the Methodist Church. However, all traditional denominations are experiencing a decline in Britain. The Covid-19 pandemic has seen an increasing number of churches closing for worship. People got out of the habit of attending worship or recognised that they could no longer carry all the responsibilities they had in their churches.

In this final study, we will focus on whether we hold to a form of religion without the Holy Spirit's power. Have we become 'do it yourself' churches without the renewing, enabling power of the Holy Spirit? There are plenty of programmes for change and growth available to us. Yet, are we ready to pay the cost in prayer, obedience to Scripture and inviting Jesus to be Lord of every aspect of our lives?

We will focus on three Old Testament passages, challenging the reader to return to a renewed relationship with God and releasing the rivers of living water.

Re-digging The Wells (Genesis 26:12-33)

In 2012, Karen and I visited Jordan and Egypt. We crossed the wilderness close to Sinai. We saw the importance of the wells for the Bedouin who lived there. It gave context to the events of Genesis 26:12-33, where Isaac's family, servants, herds, and flocks were moving from place to place in search of water. Isaac inherited flocks and herds from his father, Abraham. As the flocks and herds increased, the pressure on land and water increased, resulting in conflict with the Philistines, who had provided hospitality for Isaac. The Philistines filled in the wells that Abraham's servants had dug so that Isaac, with his flocks and herds, had to move on. Isaac moved away to the Valley of Gerar and settled there. Isaac began to reopen the wells dug by Abraham to provide for the people, herds and flocks. Isaac named the wells Esek, Sitnah and Rehoboth. The names of the wells describe what happened in each place. Esek means dispute where the herders of Gerah claimed, *'The water is ours.'* Sitnah means opposition, where the local herders again quarrelled over water rights. Finally, Isaac's servant dug another well named Rehoboth, which means room. There was no dispute with the local herders, so Isaac settled there.

 Eventually, they went to Beersheba. Here God made a covenant with Isaac.

> *'I am the God of your father Abraham. Do not be afraid, for I am with you; I will bless you and will increase the number of your descendants for the sake of my servant Abraham'* (Genesis 26:24).

Beersheba can have two meanings: 'well of the oath' referring to the covenant between God and Isaac or 'well of seven' referring to the wells in that place.

Looking at this passage from a spiritual viewpoint, we learn important lessons. In the Bible, wells often symbolise blessings from the Lord. Those blessings, however, are often lost due to dispute and opposition or renewed by restoring the covenant relationship with God.

The Philippian church had a rich heritage. Paul's letter rejoiced in the mission and growth of the church. However, he noted that a dispute had arisen between Euodia and Syntyche, who had been Paul's co-workers and worked hard for the gospel (Philippians 4:2-3). Paul sought to nip the conflict in the bud and restore the friendship between the two ladies. There was a call for reconciliation.

Churches can split over the slightest thing. Opposition occurs, and people are hurt. From Genesis to the present day, we can cite occasions when that has happened. Prominent members or ministers are in a strained relationship and move on. Rumours abound where facts are not made known. It damages the individuals, the fellowship in the church and the mission to the community. Disputes and disobedience are the equivalent of *'filling them* (the wells) *with earth'* (Genesis 26:15). Where such things happen, churches need a ministry of reconciliation. We should always look to put right the hurts that occur to release the flow of life-giving water.

There are also occasions where an individual or groups of people experience spiritual renewal. The wider church fellowship, rather than encouraging them, dampen their enthusiasm and desire to grow in faith and share that faith and engage in mission. It is sad to see this happen.

Often churches keep looking for something new when all we need to do is to re-dig the old wells of spiritual life that God's people have depended on from the beginning. Whenever there has been a revival in the church, it's been because somebody has re-dug the old wells releasing God's life-giving Spirit. The Northumbria Community follow a pattern of daily prayer, with 'readings from writers and thinkers down through the ages, to help the modern pilgrim find solid ground in their daily walk with God' (Celtic Daily Prayer, Collins, 2005).

In our Methodist history, when John Wesley heard the preface of Luther's commentary on Romans at a quarter before nine on 24 May 1738, his heart was strangely warmed. He found the well of justification by faith again and began to preach faith in Jesus for the forgiveness of sin. The calling upon the Methodist Church is to spread Scriptural holiness throughout the land.

Discovering the original vision for a church plant, 10, 50 even 150 years ago, can help the church to recognise the vision for the future. I share some reflections from my ministry.

In my first appointment, a church plant on Colshaw Estate was down to the faithful few worshipping on a Sunday, morning and evening. The Bramhall Circuit and St Chad's Parish Church supported the church. Colshaw was and still is an area of need, surrounded by great affluence. The church began with help from Poynton Baptist Church when Manchester City Council built an overspill estate between Handforth and Wilmslow in the late 60s and 70s. The work started by busing people to local churches. Then a vacant shop became the home for children's work, a food bank, worship, prayer and discipleship groups. However, the land saved for the Handforth by-pass had cut off the church from the estate. In the mid-1990s, the Dean Row shopping centre, including a new community centre, was built. Bill Short, a retired businessman from St Chad's, worked hard to ensure the church was at the heart of that community centre. The community asked me to chair the planning group and the community centre. The church became Christ Church Colshaw, a Local Ecumenical Partnership and moved into the new centre. The focus was Sunday worship, Toddlers Group, evening children's group and food bank. Over the next few years, the church grew. Thirty years later, the church continues to fulfil its original vision to support that community and make disciples.

Recently, in the Liverpool South Circuit, Princes Park and Elm Hall Drive Methodist Churches have renewed their mission statements, having articulated the original vision for the planting of both churches. Princes Park has always been a place of welcome for people arriving in Liverpool from the various countries in Africa and the Caribbean. Other churches have been planted in Liverpool and beyond for people sharing the same language or culture, who found a welcome at Princes Park. Princes Park is now home to various language fellowship groups. Since the decision to remain open in Autumn 2021 several people have begun to worship with us. Others pop in for fellowship and prayer when the church door is open. Alongside the church is the Methodist Centre, providing invaluable work for black youngsters. A new chapter is emerging in the life of Princes Park Methodist Church.

In considering its future, Elm Hall Drive was reminded of the founding vision of those who planted the church. It was to serve the new housing around Penny Lane. As the church reviews the mission statement and feasibility studies, there is a renewed call to serve that area.

Princes Park and Elm Hall Drive churches were both considering their future. It would have been so easy to call time, shut the door and move to another church. It is much harder to continue, repair the buildings, take up our spades, re-dig the wells of our inheritance and reclaim the calling of our forebears. It will be interesting to discover what happens. In a joint service in January 2022 for both congregations, I pointed out three elements of the calling that they share.

First, we are called to serve our communities. They are very different, with different needs. Still, both our communities need a vibrant witness to the saving and healing power of Jesus. Have you noticed what has happened since we made that decision? God has led people through our doors needing a home, a conversation and an expression of God's love and care.

Secondly, we are called to serve displaced people. Princes Park has been a spiritual home for displaced people from Africa and the Caribbean. We provide a home for La Manne Cachée Church, a French-speaking Congolese congregation. Elm Hall Drive has also been a place for displaced people, students from all over the world, and now our Tamil congregation. In both churches, many have moved on to leadership positions in other churches.

Thirdly, we are called to offer Christ the living water to a thirsty generation. When Jesus spoke with the woman at Jacob's well in Sychar, he noticed her thirst. *'Everyone who drinks of this water will be thirsty again, but whoever drinks the water I give to him will become in him a spring of water welling up to eternal life'* (John 4:13). In every congregation, there are needs. There are deep hurts, unforgiven sin, a longing to be accepted and loved. Jesus was getting to the deep need of the woman who had looked for and not experienced true love. Jesus offered her the love she needed. She experienced love, acceptance, forgiveness, purpose, and a place in the family of God. When we preach the cross, we release the power of God's love into people's lives. As people respond to the love of God, they are overwhelmed with love, peace, and joy. We need to remove our timidity and have the courage to share our stories of God's love for us.

When we dig back into our history, we discover why each congregation was formed. When we reclaim that calling, we begin to see evidence of the reopened well of renewal and the waters of the Holy Spirit's blessing and healing flowing in our mission and ministry.'

For Reflection...

4.4. What was the original purpose of your church?

4.5. What re-digging needs to take place so that living water can flow again?

4.6. Are there any springs of living water which you need to re-dig within your own life?

God met Isaac and renewed the covenant made with Abraham. The Methodist Church has at its heart the annual Covenant Service. As we renew our relationship with God, we receive the blessing of God and are re-filled with the Holy Spirit.

Return to the Springs of Living Water (Jeremiah 2:13)

Jeremiah was known as the weeping prophet. He delivered God's judgement on the nation, preparing them for exile. In Jeremiah 2:13, God proclaims, *'My people have committed two sins: They have forsaken me, the spring of living water, and have dug their own cisterns, broken cisterns that cannot hold water.'*

God's damning judgement is upon a people who have turned Baal and other gods rather than following him. They have forsaken the spring of living water, following other gods who cannot help or sustain them. They are man-made cisterns which are broken and cannot hold water.

Jesus cried at the Festival of Tabernacles, *'Let anyone who is thirsty come to me and drink. Whoever believes in me, as Scripture has said, rivers of living water will flow from within them'* (John 7:37-38). We must respond to the invitation. All the programmes in the world will not replace responding to Jesus' invitation.

Rivers of Living Water Flow for the Healing of the Nations (Ezekiel 47:1-12)

Ezekiel was the prophet who was with the exiled people in Babylon. God called Ezekiel to be a prophet to the exiles and those left in Jerusalem. It perhaps surprised Ezekiel that he had a vision of God by the rivers of Babylon. God was with him and those in exile. God called Ezekiel to share visions and prophecies with the people, even though the people would not listen.

Even though in Babylon, there is a focus on the temple in Jerusalem. He observes the priests worshipping other gods and doing things detestable to God. In Ezekiel 10, God's glory departs from the temple. The fall of Jerusalem follows. However, for all the messages of judgement, there are also messages of hope. Ezekiel sees the temple rebuilt, the priesthood and the nation restored, and the glory of God return to the temple. God will breathe new life into Israel and restoration will occur (Ezekiel 34-46).

There then follows a most striking picture of a river flowing from under the threshold of the temple, in ever-increasing depth, bringing life even to the Dead Sea, and providing fruit around the year and leaves for the healing of the nations

(Ezekiel 47:1-12). It is a beautiful picture of renewal for the land and Israel.

This image may have been part of the message issued by Jesus at the Festival of Tabernacles. The gift of the Holy Spirit proceeds from the Father and the Son, fills, and flows through the believers.

The increasing depth means you can paddle, wade, or go with the river's flow. Are we willing to take our feet off the floor and trust the Holy Spirit to bring renewal to our church and communities? Do we see that God wants to bring life and healing to his broken world?

By his breath in the valley of dry bones (Ezekiel 37:1-14), God raises a defeated nation to new life. *'I will put my Spirit in you, and you will live, and I will settle you in your own land. Then you will know that I the Lord have spoken, and I have done it, declares the Lord'* (Ezekiel 37:14). By the river of life (Ezekiel 47:1-12), God brings new life to the nation and creation. The picture begins with the breath of life and continues with the river of life. Is this foreshadowing the coming of the Holy Spirit as breath on Easter Day and river at Pentecost?

Spiritual renewal for the disciples began on Easter Evening with the peace of the Holy Spirit and continued at Pentecost with the power of the Holy Spirit. Spiritual renewal is the revitalisation of Christians, renewing our love for Jesus and others. Spiritual renewal is receiving the power of the Holy Spirit to bring the gospel of salvation, hope and healing to families, friends and communities.

Spiritual renewal is available to all who ask. Jesus has promised this. His promises never fail!

1. Come down, O Love divine!
seek out this soul of mine
and visit it with your own ardour glowing;
O Comforter, draw near,
within my heart appear,
and kindle it, your holy flame bestowing.

2. There let it freely burn
till earthly passions turn
to dust and ashes in its heat consuming;
and let your glorious light
shine ever on my sight,
and make my pathway clear, by your illuming.

3. Let holy charity
my outward vesture be,
and lowliness become my inner clothing;
true lowliness of heart
which takes the humbler part,
and for its own shortcomings weeps with loathing.

4. And so the yearning strong
with which the soul will long
shall far surpass the power of human telling;
for none can guess its grace
till we become the place
in which the Holy Spirit makes his dwelling.

Bianco da Siena trans Richard Littledale
Singing the Faith 372